Analysing Financial Statements

in a week

ROGER MASON

Hodder & Stoughton

A MEMBER OF THE HODDER HEADLINE GROUP

Orders: please contact Bookpoint Ltd, 130 Milton Park, Abingdon, Oxon
OX14 4SB.
Telephone: (44) 01235 827720, Fax: (44) 01235 400454. Lines are open from
9.00–6.00, Monday to Saturday, with a 24 hour message answering service.
Email address: orders@bookpoint.co.uk

British Library Cataloguing in Publication Data
A catalogue record for this title is available from The British Library

ISBN 0 340 856122

First published 2002
Impression number   10 9 8 7 6 5 4 3 2 1
Year   2007 2006 2005 2004 2003 2002

Copyright © 2002 Roger Mason

Typeset by SX Composing DTP, Rayleigh, Essex.
Printed in Great Britain for Hodder & Stoughton Educational, a division of
Hodder Headline Plc, 338 Euston Road, London NW1 3BH. by
Cox & Wyman Ltd, Reading, Berkshire.

The leading organisation for professional management

As the champion of management, the Chartered Management Institute shapes and supports the managers of tomorrow. By sharing intelligent insights and setting standards in management development, the Institute helps to deliver results in a dynamic world.

Setting and raising standards

The Institute is a nationally accredited organisation, responsible for setting standards in management and recognising excellence through the award of professional qualifications.

Encouraging development, improving performance

The Institute has a vast range of development programmes, qualifications, information resources and career guidance to help managers and their organisations meet new challenges in a fast-changing environment.

Shaping opinion

With in-depth research and regular policy surveys of its 91,000 individual members and 520 corporate members, the Chartered Management Institute has a deep understanding of the key issues. Its view is informed, intelligent and respected.

For more information call 01536 204222 or visit www.managers.org.uk

C O N T E N T S

There has never been a time when managers, and indeed people in general, were more exposed to a multitude of financial statements than they are today. To take just one example, millions of people are investors and are sent accounts and financial information relating to the companies in which they invest. Even non-financial managers are often involved in budgeting and regular financial reporting. They are expected to understand the accounts put in front of them and to contribute to the analysis and interpretation of the figures.

It is important that managers understand the principles of analysing accounts. They will then be able to deal with such questions as:

* Is our customer in trouble? Are we going to be paid?
* Profits are down – why exactly?
* Just what is gearing? And does it matter?

This book is written for managers wishing to answer these questions. By setting aside a little time each day for a week, you will greatly increase your understanding of accounts and how to analyse them. Finally, some practical advice. It will be of great help if you get hold of a set of accounts, and analyse them, as explained in this book. It is likely to be more meaningful if the accounts are for a company that you know well, such as your employer. Obtaining copies of accounts is not difficult and on Wednesday we explain how it can be done.

The right approach

The analysis of financial statements is very much a hands-on, practical matter and much of the rest of the week is devoted to hands-on, practical examples. However, you will get the best results if you have some clear ideas about the benefits and the best ways to set about the analysis. You should also know about the many traps that lie in wait. Our programme today is:

- The benefits of analysing financial statements
- The best methods to adopt
- Traps to avoid

The benefits of analysing financial statements

You may well think that the benefits are self-evident and, to some extent, they probably are. Nevertheless, it is worth thinking about because one or two advantages may have escaped you. The following are three of the most important:

A big step towards effective management

Effective management should be based on knowledge of the facts and the trends. Furthermore, effective management should be based on a comprehensive understanding of the facts and the trends. Without this, managers may act in a way that is inappropriate or has harmful consequences. Effective analysis of financial statements should help managers to get things right.

Help to ensure that wise investment and commercial decisions are made

Both investment and management involve many choices. Effective analysis should help to make the right decisions.

Help to reduce the losses caused by bad debts

When a company becomes insolvent, it is almost always found that published financial information had given warnings of the impending disaster. In particular, deteriorating performance and liquidity has usually been revealed. The published information needs analysis and interpretation, and the rewards for doing so can be great.

The best methods to adopt

Sometimes the analysis and conclusions will be so obvious that they almost jump out of the page at you. More often they have to be unearthed with diligent and skilful work. You should take care even when the conclusions seem obvious. There are a lot of traps and certain factors should make you doubt the obvious interpretation. Some of these traps are explained later in this chapter. For the best results you should keep the following points in mind.

Look for an explanation

There may be a good reason for an apparently bad figure. For example, a major advertising campaign at the end of a financial period may reduce profits in the short term, despite holding the promise of increasing sales and profits in the next period.

Ask the question 'What am I comparing it with?'

Most of the information is much more meaningful if it is compared with something. So compare it. Useful questions to ask include:

- How does it compare with last year?
- How does it compare with the industry average?
- Is it better or worse than budget?

Be sceptical

Financial statements are prepared according to rules and assumptions. If different rules and assumptions are used, then different results will be obtained. Published financial statements may legitimately, within certain limits, use different rules and assumptions, which in most cases must be stated. There are only self-imposed restraints relating to data prepared for internal management purposes.

In some cases the correct profit is a matter of opinion and this can be true of many of the assets and liabilities. Cash, though, is almost entirely a matter of fact. It is there or it is not there. You should always approach your examination in a sceptical and enquiring state of mind.

Look for the trends
It is often very useful to examine the trends because they may be much more revealing than a single figure or comparison. Fortunately, published accounts of companies must by law give corresponding figures for the previous period. A deteriorating payment performance, for example, often indicates liquidity problems, although it can also mean that selfish managers are hoarding cash at the expense of suppliers. If a company has gone from paying in 30 days to paying in 90 days, it may be more worrying than if it has consistently taken 90 days to pay.

Look at the notes and the accounting policies
You may be familiar with the saying *'the large print giveth and the small print taketh away'*. Professional analysts always spend time studying the notes to published accounts and the accounting policies. You should do the same and you should pay particular attention to any changes in accounting policies. Laws and accounting standards govern certain information that must be disclosed in the notes to published accounts of companies, and also in the directors' report.

Be open-minded
Do not have too many preconceived ideas about what you
will find. Be receptive to the unexpected.

Traps to avoid

Even experienced financial analysts can make mistakes and
fall into one of the many traps that may be encountered, and
it is more likely that someone not financially sophisticated
will do so. Below are some of the mistakes to avoid.

Not taking full account of seasonal factors
This is a common mistake. Consider a specialist greetings
card shop that commences business on 1 May. Its first two 6-
monthly profit and loss accounts are shown below.

	6 months to 31 October	6 months to 30 April
Sales in period	£300,000	£306,000
Net profit before tax	£18,000	£18,600
Profit as a percentage of sales	6.0%	6.1%

This appears to show a steady performance with the second period being very slightly better than the first. However, this is misleading. A specialist greetings card shop would expect, because of Christmas, to make at least 25 per cent of annual sales in the month of December. Valentine's Day, Easter and Mother's Day also fall in the second period. When all of this is taken into account, the results in the second period will be seen as disappointing. Of course, an alternative explanation might be that results in the first period are particularly good.

Not making allowances for trading periods having different lengths
Consider the following:

	10 months to 31 October 2001	14 months to 31 December 2002
Sales in period	£1,000,000	£1,400,000
Net profit before tax	£100,000	£140,000

Although the second period seems better, if you allow for the different lengths the results are identical, with the profit percentage being 10 per cent in each case.

Not realising that the figures have been massaged
Consider a company that usually operates with a bank overdraft. However, the managers do not pay suppliers in the last 3 weeks of the trading period in order to show no bank borrowings in the balance sheet. This is unfair to suppliers but a common practice. The balance sheet will of course show trade creditors being higher than usual.

Forgetting that some things can only be known by insiders
Published financial statements reveal a great deal, but there
are some things that can only be known by those with inside
information. Consider two companies that manufacture and
sell widgets.

	Company A	Company B
Sales	£1,000,000	£1,600,000
Cost of sales	£400,000	£720,000
Gross margin	60%	55%

Company A appears to be more efficient, but the figures
could be affected by the different accounting treatment of
certain factory costs, such as power and business rates.
Company A might treat these costs as general overheads,
whereas Company B might allocate them to production costs.
Overall net profit will of course be unaffected.

Not always comparing like with like
A recent set of accounts from Marks and Spencer plc
discloses the following:

Sales for year (in £m)	8,075.7
Trade debtors at the balance sheet date (in £m)	44.4

You can easily work out that customers take an average of
two days to pay for their purchases. The calculation is:

$$\frac{44.4}{8,075.7} \times 365 = 2.0$$

You may think that this is stunningly good, and that Marks
and Spencer must employ the world's best credit controllers.
This may or may not be true, but it should not be deduced
from these figures. The reason for this is that the great

majority of sales are made for cash. Trade debtors should really be compared with just the part of sales that are made on credit.

Now consider the widget manufacturer whose accounts disclose the following:

Sales for year £900,000
Trade debtors at the balance sheet date £100,000

This appears to show that customers take an average of 40.6 days to pay. The calculation is:

$$\frac{100,000}{900,000} \times 365 = 40.6$$

This too is probably wrong because sales will almost certainly exclude VAT and trade debtors will probably include it. If trade debtors all include 17.5 per cent VAT, the correct calculation is:

$$\frac{85,106}{900,000} \times 365 = 34.5 \text{ days}$$

Not taking note of a change in accounting policy
Consider a company that 2 years ago purchased a piece of machinery for £1 million and in the first year depreciated it by 20 per cent.

In the second year it changed its policy and depreciated it by only 10 per cent. Clearly declared net profit before tax will be £100,000 higher than if the change had not been made. Fortunately, notes to the published accounts must disclose significant changes in accounting policies and spell out the consequences.

Failing to take full account of the notes

It is sometimes said that professional analysts spend more time studying the notes to the accounts than they spend studying the actual accounts. This is wise of them because the accounts are often just the starting point. In Britain (as in nearly all other countries) the law and various accounting standards specify a great deal of information that must be disclosed in the notes to published accounts or elsewhere. The following are among the things that must be disclosed:

- Details of the company's position in a group, if this is applicable
- Details of any contingent liabilities at the balance sheet date
- Details of any capital commitments at the balance sheet date
- Details of the depreciation charge
- Total employment costs
- Details of directors' remuneration

Applying percentages to small base figures

This is best illustrated with an example. Suppose that a company has a turnover of £1,000,000 in two successive years. The profit in the first year is £100 and the profit in the second year is £200. It would be true to say that the profit had doubled, but such a claim should be viewed in the context of the very low figures involved.

Summary

We have started the week by looking at different aspects of financial analysis. The following points are especially important:

- The analysis of financial statements is a valuable management tool
- It can help to prevent bad debts
- You should not analyse in a vacuum. It is usually a good idea to compare your results with something
- Remember the saying *'The large print giveth and the small print taketh away'*
- Persevere and be open-minded
- Do not rush in – there may be traps to avoid
- On no account neglect the notes to the accounts
- Always compare like with like
- Remember that there are some things that only insiders can know

Tomorrow we will get to grips with the profit and loss account.

The profit and loss account

Nearly all businesses trade in the hope of making a profit, though not all of them actually manage to do so. The profit and loss account is always extremely important and it is an excellent place to start our study. Today's programme is:

- An example of a profit and loss account
- Profit to turnover comparison
- Cost of sales and trading profit
- Manufacturing cost and associated matters
- The sales figures
- Overheads

An example of a profit and loss account

An example of a profit and loss account is given below. It is not in a form suitable for publication but it is designed to convey key information. Comparative figures for the previous year are given which can assist anyone drawing conclusions and identifying trends. Much of this chapter consists of analysis of the example.

You will notice that the profit and loss account covers a specified period of time and that it is laid out logically with sales at the top and profit at the bottom. Sales means invoiced sales, and represents goods that have been supplied or services performed. The invoices may or may not have been paid at the end of the profit period. Sales, in this context, does not mean orders taken, which will probably be a completely different figure. Profit is expressed at different levels and this is explained later in the chapter.

Our example is a manufacturing company and manufacturing costs are separated from the overheads. It is important that only the costs of goods sold in the year appear in the profit and loss account, otherwise a misleading result would be shown. The figure of £529,006 for materials used in the goods sold is achieved by adding to purchases in the year, stock at the beginning of the year. Stock at the end of the year is deducted. You will notice that the figure of £189,498 is the closing stock for 2001 and appears again as the opening stock for 2002.

Cheviot Products Ltd
Profit and Loss Account for the Year
to 31 December 2002

	2002 £	2001 £
Sales		
Northern region	984,166	824,199
Southern region	639,278	803,241
	1,623,444	1,627,440
Cost of sales		
Stock at beginning of year	189,498	136,994
Add purchases in year	531,222	702,417
	720,720	839,411
Less stock at end of year	191,714	189,498
	529,006	649,913
Production wages	201,112	271,611
Factory rent	94,000	94,000
Power costs	67,336	66,183
Other production costs	39,231	47,662
	930,685	1,129,369
Gross profit	692,759	498,071
Overheads		
Salaries	147,181	172,613
Rent	50,000	50,000
Transport	44,298	56,347
Other	79,616	98,785
	321,095	377,745
Profit before finance charges	371,664	120,326
Less interest	96,387	108,769
Net profit before tax	275,277	11,557
Less tax charge for year	63,736	2,421
Net profit after tax	211,541	9,136

Profit to turnover comparison

This is probably the most commonly used of all the accounting ratios and it is the headline figure frequently taken to show how well or badly a business is doing. The example shows profit struck at three levels, although it is profit before tax that is most often used. Businesses sometimes show exceptional items separately and 'profit before exceptional items' is a fourth possibility. This will be examined when we look at published accounts later in the week. The calculations for Cheviot Products Ltd are as follows:

Using 'Profit before finance charges'

Current year is $\dfrac{371,664}{1,623,444} = 22.9\%$

Previous year is $\dfrac{120,326}{1,627,440} = 7.4\%$

Using 'Net profit before tax'

Current year is $\dfrac{275,277}{1,623,444} = 17.0\%$

Previous year is $\dfrac{11,557}{1,627,440} = 0.7\%$

Using 'Net profit after tax'

Current year is $\dfrac{211,541}{1,623,444} = 13.0\%$

Previous year is $\dfrac{9,136}{1,627,440} = 0.6\%$

Of course calculating the percentages is only the first stage.
You must now give some thought to what the figures mean,
and there are two important questions to be answered.

1 *Is it a good result?* You must decide this for yourself and
   your answer may be influenced by factors such as your
   expectations, the budget, the performance of competitors
   and the return on capital employed or return on
   investment (ROCE or ROI). This last term is explained on
   Thursday. However, that said, the answer may be 'yes'.
   Many managers would be satisfied with a net profit before
   tax of 17 per cent of turnover.

2 *Do the figures show a satisfactory trend?* It would be better if
   more than one previous year was available for
   comparison, but there has been a large and obvious
   improvement in the figures. Cheviot Products Ltd has
   moved from a position not much better then break even to
   what appears to be a satisfactory profit. A study of further
   previous years would reveal whether the current year is

unusual or whether for some reason the previous year was not typical.

It is sometimes said that death and taxes are the only two certainties in life. An internal profit and loss account may be prepared without showing a deduction for the tax charge (or possibly an addition for the tax credit), but this will certainly be included in published accounts. Many people prefer to base their analysis on pre-tax profits but the tax charge may be a significant factor. Comparable businesses are taxable under the same laws and tax rates, but it would be a mistake to assume that their tax charges will be a uniform percentage of their turnover. Effective tax planning and individual circumstances may make a significant difference. Unless you work for the tax authorities, a low tax charge is cause for satisfaction.

Cost of sales and trading profit

These principles are best studied in a business that just buys and sells, like a retail shop, whereas the company used in the example is a manufacturing company. The following example shows how the calculations are done.

	£	£
Sales		100,000
Stock at beginning of year	33,000	
Add purchases in year	47,000	
	80,000	

Less stock at end of year	32,000	
Cost of sales		48,000
Trading profit		52,000

The method of calculation eliminates timing differences and ensures that only the cost of goods actually sold is brought into the profit and loss account. The cost of goods not yet sold is retained as an asset in the balance sheet. Counting and correctly valuing the stock must be done carefully and lost or damaged stock must be written off. In this example the cost of goods sold is:

$$\frac{48,000}{100,000} = 48.0\%$$

The gross margin is:

$$\frac{52,000}{100,000} = 52.0\%$$

This is the amount that is available to pay for the overheads and interest and, after deducting these costs, will be the net profit before tax.

Whether or not 52.0 per cent is a satisfactory margin will depend on management policy and the nature of the business. Some managers, like the late Mr Jack Cohen who founded Tesco, have a successful policy of *'pile it high and sell it cheap'*. They aim to buy volume with cheap prices. Other managers prefer to maintain a wide margin.

You will realise that there are two possible ways of improving the gross margin. It can be done by raising selling prices or achieving lower purchasing prices.

Manufacturing cost and associated matters

Our example company, Cheviot Products Ltd, is a manufacturing company. This means that it buys in raw materials or components (or both) and turns them into finished products. It follows that items such as the salaries of production workers and factory power costs must be added before the manufacturing cost is known. Different businesses may have different accounting policies concerning the allocation of costs and this can complicate comparisons. An obvious problem in the Cheriot Products Ltd example is the £94,000 for factory rent. Another business may appear more efficient because it owns its factory and therefore has no expense under this heading. This is an example of why it is necessary to check that you are comparing like with like.

The calculations for manufacturing cost as a percentage of sales are as follows:

Current year is $\dfrac{930,685}{1,623,444} = 57.3\%$

Previous year is $\dfrac{1,129,369}{1,627,440} = 69.4\%$

The calculations for the gross profit margin are as follows:

Current year is $\dfrac{692,759}{1,623,444} = 42.7\%$

Previous year is $\dfrac{498,071}{1,627,440} = 30.6\%$

As with the previous section you should not have fixed ideas about what is a good result and what is a poor result. It depends on many factors and will vary from sector to sector.

There has clearly been a big change between the two years and this goes a long way towards explaining the overall improvement in profit. Much of this is due to outside purchasing. The cost/sales ratio has moved from

$$\frac{649,913}{1,627,440} = 39.9\% \quad \text{to} \quad \frac{529,006}{1,623,444} = 32.6\%$$

The other favourable change is production wages which has moved from

$$\frac{271,611}{1,627,440} = 16.7\% \quad \text{to} \quad \frac{201,112}{1,623,444} = 12.4\%$$

The sales figures

At first sight there is not much to say about the sales figures. This is partly because total sales are almost the same year on year and partly because so many other things are compared with them. However, the split between the two regions looks interesting.

	Current year	Previous year
Northern region	60.6%	50.6%
Southern region	39.4%	49.4%

The increase in sales in the northern region, both relative and absolute, may be of little significance, but it may be of great importance. A person using the profit and loss account for management control purposes should certainly be prompted to ask some questions.

Overheads

Our analysis of the profit and loss account of Cheviot Products Ltd concludes with an examination of the overheads. As a percentage of sales they are:

Current year is $\dfrac{321,095}{1,623,444} = 19.8\%$

Previous year is $\dfrac{377,745}{1,627,440} = 23.2\%$

There has been a favourable movement between the two periods and this is a contributing factor to the overall profit improvement.

Practical questions

(The answers to this section are given at the end of the book.)

The day concludes with an opportunity for you to test your understanding of how profit and loss accounts may be analysed. The profit and loss account of Broadland Timber Benches Ltd is below and it is followed by six practical questions.

Broadland Timber Benches Ltd
Profit and Loss Account for the Year
to 31 December 2002

	2002 £	2001 £
Sales		
UK	4,176,113	4,231,668
Export	3,961,258	2,009,784
	8,137,371	6,241,452
Cost of sales		
Stock at beginning of year	623,147	634,298
Add purchases in year	6,900,284	3,467,998
	7,523,431	4,102,296
Less stock at end of year	1,200,146	623,147
	6,323,285	3,479,149
Gross profit	1,814,086	2,762,303
Overheads		
Salaries and associated costs	631,842	541,316
Transport costs	98,334	68,770
Rent and property taxes	152,664	99,800
Maintenance	31,191	24,221
Electricity	34,778	25,072
Publicity	553,615	310,668
All other	71,012	41,279
	1,573,436	1,111,126
Profit before finance charges	240,650	1,651,177
Less interest	221,389	47,662
Net profit before tax	19,261	1,603,515
Less tax charge for year	5,112	429,276
Profit after tax	14,149	1,174,239

1 What is the percentage after tax return on total sales in the year to 31 December 2002?
2 Expressed as a percentage, what is the change in the gross margin between 2001 and 2002?
3 What proportion of total sales in each year comprises exports?
4 To what extent, if at all, has the increase in overheads contributed to the decline in profitability?
5 Suggest three main reasons for the reduction in profits between the two years.
6 Has the increase in exports been a failure?

Summary

The profit and loss account is one of the two main financial statements. We have:

- Looked at how a profit and loss account is laid out
- Seen how profit is compared with turnover, using three different levels of profit
- Looked at the significance of cost of sales and of manufacturing cost
- Examined sales figures and overheads

Tomorrow we move on to the other main financial statement – the balance sheet.

The balance sheet

The balance sheet is the second of the two main financial statements. It fulfils a completely different function from the profit and loss account and it is very important.Today we shall look at:

- An example of a balance sheet
- Liquidity analysis
- Gearing
- Stock turn
- Debtor days outstanding
- Creditor days outstanding

An example of a balance sheet

An example of a balance sheet is given below, with the corresponding figures for the previous year given after that. The comparative figures are essential for an analyst who wants to plot trends. Much of this chapter consists of analysis of these examples. These are company balance sheets but are not accompanied by notes and are not in a form suitable for publication. Published balance sheets with notes will be studied later in the week.

You will notice that a balance sheet reflects the position at a stated date. This is unlike a profit and loss account, which covers trading activity over a period of time, often a year. A balance sheet is like a snapshot; different figures would be shown if it were dated a day earlier or a day later.

As the name implies, a balance sheet balances and the figures, in pre-computer days at least, are listed on a sheet of paper. The profit and loss account for the period leading up to the balance sheet date is closed off and the profit (or loss) is transferred to reserves. This is after paying or reserving tax and (if appropriate) dividends. A balance sheet is a listing of every balance in the bookkeeping system which, given the essentials of a double entry system, explains why it balances.

The result reveals much about the position of the business on the given date. Of course, not every account is listed individually. They are grouped in a logical manner. The balance sheet shows two identical totals. One represents the net assets (total assets less total liabilities). The other represents the total funds invested in the business by the owners. In the case of a company this is share capital and reserves.

Haggleton Ltd
Balance Sheet for the Year to 31 December 2002

	£	£
Fixed assets		
Freehold property	1,012,396	
Plant and machinery	2,317,588	
Motor vehicles	124,601	
Fixtures and fittings	103,275	
		3,557,860
Current assets		
Stock	1,617,593	
Trade debtors	2,001,882	
Prepayments	169,317	
Unlisted investments	44,357	
	3,833,149	
Current liabilities		
Trade creditors	962,444	
Taxation	291,387	
Bank overdraft	1,736,429	
Accruals	206,394	
	3,196,654	
		636,495
Creditors: bank loan falling due after more than 1 year		(500,000)
		3,694,355
Capital and reserves		
Ordinary shares		400,000
Preference shares		1,000,000
Profit and loss account		2,294,355
		3,694,355

Haggleton Ltd
Balance Sheet for the Year to 31 December 2001

	£	£
Fixed assets		
Freehold property	1,012,396	
Plant and machinery	1,849,218	
Motor vehicles	122,776	
Fixtures and fittings	106,197	
		3,090,587
Current assets		
Stock	1,711,496	
Trade debtors	1,883,197	
Prepayments	156,317	
Unlisted investments	44,357	
	3,795,367	
Current liabilities		
Trade creditors	1,001,293	
Taxation	230,022	
Bank overdraft	2,941,166	
Accruals	198,427	
	4,370,908	
		(575,541)
Creditors: bank loan falling		
due after more than 1 year		–
		2,515,046
Capital and reserves		
Ordinary shares		400,000
Preference shares		–
Profit and loss account		2,115,046
		2,515,046

Liquidity analysis

Companies are not forced into involuntary liquidation because they are not making profits, although this is extremely unhelpful. It is, perhaps surprisingly, common for companies to go into liquidation that are trading profitably at the time. This is particularly true of companies that have expanded rapidly. The immediate cause of business failure is usually that they run out of liquid resources and cannot pay their debts as they become due. A balance sheet will reveal vital information about working capital and liquid resources, and it is possible that impending problems may be predicted.

A balance sheet should (and a published balance sheet must) separate assets capable of being turned into cash quickly from assets held for the long term. The former are called current assets. Similarly, a balance sheet should separate liabilities payable in the short term – current liabilities – from those payable in the long term. The dividing point is usually one year.

LIQUIDITY ANALYSIS

The difference between current assets and current liabilities is the working capital. This is sometimes called net current assets, or net current liabilities if the liabilities are greater. The working capital of Haggleton Ltd is:

Working capital

| **Current year 2002** | £636,495 positive |
| **Previous year 2001** | £575,541 negative |

To put it another way, in the current year current assets are 120 per cent of current liabilities. In the previous year current assets were 87 per cent of current liabilities.

As with other balance sheet analysis, the relationship is often expressed in the form of a ratio. For the current year it is 1.2 to 1 and for the previous year it was 0.87 to 1. This is known as the current ratio.

Another frequently used ratio is the so-called quick ratio or acid test. This is more demanding than the working capital calculation because only debtors, investments, bank and cash are used, and the total of these is compared with the total of current liabilities. Only the most liquid of the current assets are brought into the calculation. Stock is excluded because it almost always takes longer to turn into cash than debtors. The quick test calculations are as follows:

Quick test

Current year 2002 $\dfrac{2,046,239}{3,196,654} = 64\%$ or 0.64 to 1

Previous year 2001 $\dfrac{1,927,554}{4,370,908} = 44\%$ or 0.44 to 1

It would be better to have some knowledge of the company before deciding whether or not the ratios for Haggleton Ltd are worrying. It might be part of a well-financed group of companies, and customers may be virtually guaranteed to pay within seven days of invoice date without being asked. On the other hand, the company may have been only 24 hours away from the bank calling in the overdraft. That said, the position at 31 December 2001 does indicate cause for concern. The working capital ratio was only 87 per cent and in many companies this would be very worrying. The quick ratio was even worse at an alarming 44 per cent.

The company obviously addressed the problem and by 31 December 2002 it had taken on a £500,000 long-term loan, which is not classed as a current liability. It had also issued £1,000,000 of new capital in the form of preference shares. A further point to note is the significant fall in the fixed assets, which must have been caused by depreciation or asset sales. Depreciation is a non-cash charge against the profit and loss account.

Gearing

The purpose of this ratio is to compare the long-term finance provided by the banks and other lenders with finance invested by the owners of the business. In the case of a company this is share capital plus reserves and it is the whole of the bottom section of the balance sheet. This is sometimes known as 'shareholders' funds'.

The ratio is sometimes expressed as a proportion, as in 1 to 1. Sometimes it is expressed as a percentage. The ratio 1 to 1 is usually taken as 50 per cent because borrowing is 50 per cent of the total.

HIGHLY GEARED

Gearing is much studied by banks who may not like to see a ratio of 1 to 1 (or some other such proportion) exceeded.

For Haggleton Ltd, at 31 December 2002 borrowing of £500,000 must be compared with shareholders' funds of £3,694,355. This is a gearing ratio of 0.14 to 1. There was not any long-term borrowing at 31 December 2001 and so the calculation cannot be made, although it should be noted that short-term borrowing exceeded shareholders' funds.

The higher a company is geared, the bigger the risk that is run. On the other hand, high gearing will bring greater rewards for shareholders if good profits are made. This is because the shareholders have invested relatively little in the company and the profits are a relatively high percentage of shareholders' funds. Conversely, low gearing is associated with low risks and lower potential rewards for shareholders.

The box on the next page illustrates the gearing effect with an example. Assumption A is taken from the Haggleton Ltd balance sheet at 31 December 2002. Assumption B is the same but switches £2,000,000 from the shareholders' funds to borrowing, making the company more highly geared.

	Assumption A	**Assumption B**
Borrowing	£500,000	£2,500,000
Shareholders' funds	£3,694,315	£1,694,315
Gearing	0.14 to 1	1.48 to 1
Profit in the year to 31 December 2003	£2,000,000	£1,900,000
Return on investment	$\frac{2,000,000}{3,694,315} = 54.1\%$	$\frac{1,900,000}{1,694,315} = 112.1\%$

It has obviously been an extremely good year and you will
see that the return on investment is considerably higher if the
company is highly geared. This would not have worked if a
shortage of working capital had forced the company to stop
trading during the year. Assumption B has slightly lower
profit than Assumption A because it will have been necessary
to pay interest on the extra borrowing.

Stock turn

This is the number of times that total stock is used (turned
over) in the course of a year. Normally, the higher the stock
turn the more efficiently the business is being run, though
there are dangers in keeping stock too low. There is scope for
misunderstanding and stock turn usually applies to all stock,
rather than just to finished stock. Seasonal factors can distort
the ratio, especially if the balance sheet date is not a typical
one.

Stock turn can be calculated by dividing the stock figure in the balance sheet into the cost of sales from the profit and loss account. There are two potential difficulties to keep in mind:

1 The correct cost of sales figure might not be readily apparent and some companies may put extra costs into it. Scrutiny of the notes may be helpful.
2 The result will be misleading if the balance sheet is not taken on a typical day. Seasonal or other factors may mean that it is not representative of the year as a whole.

In order to illustrate the calculation we will assume that Haggleton Ltd's cost of sales for the year to 31 December 2002 was £9,200,000 and for the year to 31 December 2001 it was £11,100,000. The stock turn calculations are as follows:

Current year $\dfrac{9,200,000}{1,617,593}$ = stock turn of 5.7

Previous year $\dfrac{11,100,000}{1,711,496}$ = stock turn of 6.5

The reduction in the stock turn would probably be seen as disappointing yet, as with so much analysis, understanding and interpretation may be necessary. What is normal for the industry? Was the change caused by a different management policy?

Debtor days outstanding

This measures the number of days (on average) allowed to customers to settle their accounts though unfortunately it might be more realistic to say that it measures the number of days' credit taken by customers, with or without permission. It is an important calculation and one that is frequently made. It is a measure of efficiency but is best considered with knowledge of the policy and the circumstances.

The method is to divide the sales figure from the profit and loss account into the trade debtors figure from the balance sheet. The result, if the profit and loss account covers an exact year, is then multiplied by 365 to express the result as a number of days. We will again assume that sales for the year to 31 December 2002 are £9,200,000 and that for the year to 31 December 2001 they are £11,100,000. The calculations are as follows:

Current year $\dfrac{2,001,882}{9,200,000} \times 365 = 79$ days

Previous year $\dfrac{1,883,197}{11,100,000} \times 365 = 62$ days

A potential problem is that the trade debtors total may include VAT in the outstanding invoices. The sales figure on the other hand may exclude VAT and we might make the serious mistake of not comparing like with like. If the current year figure of £2,001,882 includes 17.5 per cent VAT on all invoices, the correct calculation is:

Current year $\dfrac{1,703,729}{9,200,000} \times 365 = 68$ days

There is a more accurate way to calculate this and it overcomes the problem of an atypical balance sheet date, as well as the VAT difficulty. Unfortunately, it is only available if we know the monthly invoicing figures. Using assumed monthly figures for the current year it works like this:

	£	
Owing at 31 December 2002	2,001,882	
Less total December invoices	800,000	31 days
	1,201,882	
Less total November invoices	750,000	30 days
	451,882	
Less total October invoices	903,000	15 days
	NIL	76 days

The object is to calculate the number of days that an average invoice takes to be paid. £2,001,882 is the total amount owing by all customers at 31 December 2002. £800,000 of this was invoiced during December and this represents 31 days. We continue deducting the monthly invoicing totals until we get to NIL. October invoicing is approximately twice the remaining balance of £451,882 so this represents only part of October's 31 days – namely 15 days. The overall result is that on average invoices take 76 days to be paid.

Creditor days outstanding

If you have understood the principles of debtor days outstanding, you will have no trouble at all here. This is because creditor days outstanding is an exact mirror image of debtor days outstanding. It measures the period of time that the company takes (on average) to pay its suppliers' invoices. It is calculated by dividing the figure for total annual purchases from suppliers into the figure for trade creditors at the balance sheet date. The result is then multiplied by 365. A problem is that the figure for total purchases is not usually disclosed separately in the accounts and, therefore, some inside knowledge is required.

In order to illustrate the calculations we will assume that the total annual purchases from suppliers was £8,000,000 in 2002 and £8,800,000 in 2001. The calculations are:

Current year $\dfrac{962,444}{8,000,000} \times 365 = 44$ days

Previous year $\dfrac{1,001,293}{8,800,000} \times 365 = 42$ days

Once again you should consider whether or not the balance sheet date is typical of the year as a whole.

Practical questions

(The answers to this section are given at the end of the book.)

The day concludes with some practical questions for you to test your understanding of the principles explained. The following questions relate to the balance sheet of Canterbury Suppliers Ltd which is given below.

1 What is the amount of the working capital?
2 What is the quick ratio (sometimes known as the acid test)?
3 What is the gearing?
4 Does the gearing ratio give cause for alarm?
5 What is the stock turn?
6 What are the debtor days outstanding?
7 What are the creditor days outstanding?

Canterbury Supplies Ltd
Balance Sheet for the Year to 31 December 2002

	£	£
Fixed assets		
Freehold property	4,642,337	
Plant and machinery	2,249,896	
		6,892,233
Current assets		
Stock	841,784	
Trade debtors	2,396,114	
Other debtors	57,231	
	3,295,129	
Current liabilities		
Trade creditors	1,162,975	
Taxation	318,729	
Bank overdraft	1,682,143	
	3,163,847	
		131,282
Creditors: bank loan falling due after more than 1 year		(1,500,000)
		5,523,515
Capital and reserves		
Share capital		3,000,000
Revenue reserves		2,523,515
		5,523,515

NB: Other available information
1. Sales in the year to 31 December 2002 were £12,199,318.
2. Cost of sales in the year to 31 December 2002 was £7,621,389.
3. Trade debtors of £2,396,114 includes VAT of £356,869.
4. Total purchases from suppliers in the year to 31 December 2002 were £8,318,199.

Summary

The balance sheet is the second of the two main financial statements. Today, we have:

- Seen the significance of the balance sheet and how it is constructed
- Studied working capital and different forms of liquidity analysis
- Looked at the implications of the gearing ratio and how it is calculated
- Examined stock turn
- Studied debtor days outstanding and its mirror image creditor days outstanding

Tomorrow we shall deal with accounts prepared in a form suitable for publication.

Introduction to published accounts

Our work on Monday and Tuesday has given us information about analysis of both the profit and loss account and the balance sheet. We are now ready to work with published accounts and today's work is a solid grounding in this area. Today we shall cover:

- The obligation to publish accounts
- How to obtain copies of company accounts
- Audit requirements
- Summary of the content of a set of published accounts
- Outline details of the content
- Test your understanding
- An example of a set of accounts
- Do you remember Monday and Tuesday?

The obligation to publish accounts

In Britain, sole traders and general partnerships do not have to make their accounts available to the public. However, they may have to do so to their banks and to the Inland Revenue. Limited partnerships must publish their accounts and so must certain other bodies. In particular all limited companies are required by law to produce accounts and to make them available to anyone who wants to see them. Small and medium-sized companies are allowed to disclose less information, but they must publish their accounts. There are over 1,500,000 incorporated companies in Britain and so there are a great number of accounts available for inspection.

How to obtain copies of company accounts

One way is to ask the company in which you are interested. Many companies will respond favourably to a polite request. Failing this, anyone can obtain the accounts of any British company from Companies House. It is a legal requirement that all companies deliver a copy of their accounts to Companies House to be made available for public inspection and copying. A small fee is payable. Companies incorporated in England and Wales file at Cardiff and companies incorporated in Scotland file at Edinburgh. The two addresses are:

Companies House	Companies House
Crown Way	37 Castle Terrace
Maindy	Edinburgh
Cardiff	EH1 2ED
CF14 3UZ	
Tel: 0870 333 3636	Tel: 0870 333 3636

Almost all countries have an office equivalent to Companies House, and in many countries it is a requirement that companies file accounts so that they can be inspected and copied by the public.

Audit requirements

Different countries have different laws about auditing. The rules in Britain are likely to change soon, but at the time of writing all companies with an annual turnover in excess of £1,000,000 must have their accounts audited. For charitable companies the limit is lower.

The primary responsibility of an auditor is to give an opinion as to whether or not the accounts give a *'true and fair view'*. An auditor does not certify the accuracy of the figures.

Summary of the content of a set of published accounts

The accounts of British companies (other than small and medium-sized companies) will contain a minimum of the following:

- Directors' report
- Auditor's report
- Consolidated accounts (if it is a holding company)
- Profit and loss account
- Balance sheet
- Notes to the accounts
- Cash flow information

Outline details of the content

It is helpful to know your way round a set of accounts and to have a broad idea of what is likely to be found in each of the areas listed above. Here is an outline description for each of them.

Directors' report
Directors are required by law to disclose certain information. For all companies other than small companies, the list includes the following:

- Any material difference in market value of interests in land or buildings over book value at the balance sheet date
- The amount of recommended dividends
- A fair review of the development of the business and the position at the end of the period
- Details of any important developments since the year end
- The names of all persons who were directors during the year and details of directors' interests in shares or debentures at the beginning and end of the year
- The principal activities of the company and any changes during the year

There are many other requirements.

Auditor's report

This will state whether, in the opinion of the auditor, the accounts give a *'true and fair view'*. It will not certify the accuracy of the accounts. You will probably not see any audit qualifications, especially if it is a large company, but you should check. This only takes a short time and is usually a good first step. An audit qualification may be of vast importance or it may be a technicality.

Consolidated accounts

These are additional to the accounts of the company itself and they must be published if the company is a holding company. Consolidated accounts give the position of the whole group in relation to the outside world. Inter-group balances are netted off and so is the effect of inter-group trading. No profits are taken until a third-party sale is made.

Profit and loss account

You should already be familiar with this. The profit and loss account must be in a specified format and disclose specified information. Comparable figures for the previous period must be given. Exceptional items and also extraordinary items must be disclosed separately with details being given in the notes. Extraordinary items are separate from the ordinary activities of the company. Exceptional items are derived from ordinary activities but are exceptional because of their size or some other factor. Large redundancy payments following a factory closure might be an example of an exceptional item.

Balance sheet

You should already be familiar with this as well. Like the profit and loss account, it must be in a specified format and disclose specified information. Comparable figures for the previous balance sheet date must be given.

Notes to the accounts
The purpose of the notes is to give more detailed information in support of the figures in the accounts. Each note is given a number and cross-referenced to the accounts. Examples of notes include:

- A breakdown of fixed assets by category showing accumulated depreciation for each
- A breakdown of debtors into categories

Cash flow information
This is a statement that plots the movement in cash resources between two balance sheets. It identifies the net overall increase or decrease in cash and shows how it has happened. Analysts regard this as extremely important. Cynics sometimes observe that, although profit is partly a matter of opinion, cash is a matter of fact.

Test your understanding

(The answers to this section are given at the end of the book.)

Now test your understanding by jotting down the most likely place in an accounts package to find the following. Do not worry if you get some answers wrong because not everything is specifically mentioned in this chapter.

1 Details of a recommended dividend.
2 Total amount of interest paid by the company.
3 Total amount of borrowing repayable after more than one year.
4 Explanation of net increase in borrowing during the year.

5 Details of contingent liabilities.
6 Detailed breakdown of trade creditors.
7 Details of charitable and political donations.

An example of a set of accounts

The following reproduces key information from a set of
published accounts. Unfortunately, space precludes
everything being included but you will see the profit and loss
account, the balance sheet and key extracts from other
documents. We will work extensively with these accounts
during the rest of the week.

Rutland Robotics PLC
Profit and Loss Account for the Year
to 31 December 2002

	Note	Year ended 31 December 2002 £000	Year ended 31 December 2001 £000
Turnover	1	188,326	193,616
Cost of sales		(109,481)	(122,379)
Gross profit		78,845	71,237
Net operating expenses		(45,611)	(48,660)
Exceptional item	2	—	(6,199)
Operating profit		33,234	16,378
Interest payable	3	(2,716)	(3,406)
Profit on ordinary activities before taxation		30,518	12,972
Taxation on ordinary activities	4	(7,913)	(3,117)
Profit on ordinary activities after taxation		22,605	9,855
Dividends	5	(8,913)	(8,913)
Retained profit for the year		13,692	942

Rutland Robotics PLC
Balance Sheet at 31 December 2002

	Note	£000	£000
Tangible assets			
Fixed assets	6		29,062
Current assets			
Stocks	7	16,318	
Debtors	8	37,291	
Cash at bank and in hand		113	
		53,722	
Current liabilities			
Creditors: amounts			
falling due within 1 year	9	25,717	
Net current assets			28,005
Creditors: amounts			
falling due after more			
than 1 year	10		(5,091)
Net assets			51,976
Capital and reserves			
Called up share capital			20,637
Profit and loss account			31,339
			51,976

Rutland Robotics PLC
Balance Sheet at 31 December 2001

	Note	£000	£000
Tangible assets			
Fixed assets	6		29,458
Current assets			
Stocks	7	14,169	
Debtors	8	33,637	
Cash at bank and in hand		126	
		47,932	
Current liabilities			
Creditors: amounts			
falling due within 1 year	9	30,998	
Net current assets			16,934
Creditors: amounts			
falling due after more			
than 1 year	10		(8,108)
Net assets			38,284
Capital and reserves			
Called up share capital			20,637
Profit and loss account			17,647
			38,284

Extracts from notes to the accounts

1 Turnover

	2002 £000	2001 £000
a) By activity		
Industrial machinery	188,326	181,429
Consultancy services	–	12,187
	188,326	193,616
b) By geographical market		
United Kingdom	149,327	97,391
Rest of the world	38,999	96,225
	188,326	193,616

2 Exceptional item

During the year to 31 December 2001 the company closed its consultancy services division and withdrew from this activity. Redundancy and other costs associated with this decision totalled £6,199,000.

3 Interest payable

	2002 £000	2001 £000
On bank loans and overdrafts	2,600	3,209
Hire purchase interest	116	197
	2,716	3,406

4 Taxation on ordinary activities

	2002 £000	2001 £000
UK corporation tax		
Current year	7,926	3,177
Prior years	88	—
Deferred tax	(101)	(60)
	7,913	3,117

5 Dividends

	2002 £000	2001 £000
Ordinary shares		
· Interim dividend of 30.0p per share (last year 30.0p)	6,191	6,191
· Proposed final dividend of 13.2p per share (last year 13.2p)	2,722	2,722
	8,913	8,913

6 Tangible fixed assets

	Freehold land and buildings £000	Plant and machinery £000	Fixtures and fittings £000	Total £000
Cost or valuation				
At 31.12.01	20,500	9,731	1,438	31,669
Additions	—	2,842	201	3,043
Disposals	—	(990)	(89)	(1,079)
At 31.12.02	20,500	11,583	1,550	33,633

Depreciation

At 31.12.01	615	1,200	396	2,211
Charge for year	410	1,951	151	2,512
On disposals	—	(111)	(41)	(152)
At 31.12.02	1,025	3,040	506	4,571

Net book value				
at 31.12.02	19,475	8,543	1,044	29,062
Net book value				
at 31.12.01	19,885	8,531	1,042	29,458

7 Stocks

	2002 £000	2001 £000
Raw materials and consumables	1,977	2,038
Work in progress	4,836	6,119
Finished goods and goods for resale	9,505	6,012
	16,318	14,169

8 Debtors

	2002 £000	2001 £000
Trade debtors	35,406	31,608
Other debtors	1,486	1,597
Prepayments and accrued income	399	432
	37,291	33,637

9 Creditors: amounts falling due within one year

	2002 £000	2001 £000
Bank loan and overdraft	2,750	8,691
Trade creditors	10,241	13,629
Taxation and social security	990	1,320
Corporation tax	7,708	3,241
Obligations under hire purchase contracts	491	499
Other creditors	314	397
Proposed final dividend	2,722	2,722
Accruals	501	499
	25,717	30,998

10 Creditors: amounts falling due after more than one year

	2002 £000	2001 £000
Bank loan	4,772	7,282
Obligations under hire purchase contracts	319	826
	5,091	8,108

11 Directors

	2002 £000	2001 £000
Remuneration for management services	1,411	963
Pension contributions	506	107
	1,917	1,070

(In practice more information than this would be given.)

12 Staff numbers and costs

The average number of persons employed by the company (including directors) was as follows:

	2002	2001
Factory	702	798
Administration, sales and other	320	461
Consultancy services	—	68
	1,022	1,327

The aggregate payroll costs of these persons (including directors) was as follows:

	2002 £000	2001 £000
Wages and salaries	31,662	34,221
Social security costs	2,727	2,982
	34,389	37,203

13 Contingent liability

A United States customer has notified the company of its intention to claim damages of $50,000,000 for alleged consequential loss resulting from alleged faulty parts supplied by this company. The directors believe that the claim has no validity whatsoever and no provision has been made in these accounts.

14 Capital commitments

	2002 £000	2001 £000
Contracted but not provided for	4,219	1,203

Extract from directors' report

Last year's decision to close our consultancy services division was a painful one but the anticipated benefits were achieved. We now intend to rapidly expand our successful core business and confidently hope to double both turnover and profits within the next 2 years.

Extracts from the auditor's report

An amount of £46,938 in respect of a deposit held in a Nigerian bank account is included in 'Cash at bank and in hand' in the balance sheet. It has not been possible to obtain independent verification concerning this balance.

In our opinion the financial statements give a true and fair view of the state of the company's affairs as at 31 December 2002 and of its result for the year then ended and have been properly prepared in accordance with the Companies Act 1985.

Do you remember Monday and Tuesday?

(The answers to this section are given at the end of the book.)

The following questions should give you no trouble at all, because the principles were studied on Monday and Tuesday. Please use the 2001 accounts of Rutland Robotics PLC from today's chapter.

1 What is the working capital?
2 What is the quick ratio (acid test)?
3 What is the ratio of profit before tax to turnover?
4 What is the ratio of net operating expenses to turnover?

Summary

Our work for the rest of the week will be a little more advanced and we have paved the way for this with a thorough introduction to published accounts. Today we have:

- Seen which organisations must publish their accounts and seen how to obtain copies
- Looked at the legal requirements to have the figures audited
- Seen what must be included in the published accounts of companies and looked at each part in more detail
- Set out in full the key parts of a set of company accounts
- Tested your understanding with two different sets of questions

Tomorrow we shall analyse the accounts that are included in this chapter.

Working with published accounts

Today we shall venture more deeply into the analysis of published accounts. We will frequently refer to the accounts of Rutland Robotics PLC and you will need to keep looking at yesterday's chapter. We shall cover:

- The auditor's report
- Return on capital employed
- Exceptional items
- The profit and loss account
- Turnover analysis
- Interest cover
- Taxation
- Dividend cover

The auditor's report

This should not take long and it is a very good place to start. Auditors are required to state whether or not in their opinion the accounts give *'a true and fair view'*. They usually do say this, not least because a contrary opinion is a serious matter and not in the interests of the company or its directors. You may find a minor or technical qualification and, if so, you will need to decide how important it is and whether or not further enquiries are necessary.

The report on Rutland Robotics PLC does give the all-important assurance about a true and fair view. However, it does draw your attention to a matter of possible concern. It is suggested that this should be noted but that not too much attention need be paid.The sum of £46,938 probably seems significant to you, but it is not significant in relation to the company's profit and net worth.

Return on capital employed

This is often abbreviated to ROCE and is sometimes given the alternative name of 'Return on Investment' or ROI. It is a test much used by investors and many people consider it to be the most important of all the ratios.

ROCE is profit expressed as a percentage of the net value of the money invested in the company. Capital employed is the balance sheet total consisting of share capital plus reserves. Sometimes profit before tax is used and sometimes profit after tax is used. Exceptional items may be included or excluded. It is for you to select the definition of profit, then apply it consistently. This is especially important when you are comparing different periods or the results for different companies. ROCE can sometimes lead to embarrassing questions to company directors such as: *'Your company is achieving a return on capital employed of less than 2 per cent, but my building society gives me over 4 per cent. Why don't we sell up and put the money in the building society?'*

Using 'Profit after exceptional items and after tax,' ROCE for Rutland Robotics PLC is:

	Current year	**Previous year**
Profit (in £000s)	22,605	9,855
Capital employed (in £000s)	51,976	38,284
Return on captial employed	43.5%	25.7%

By most standards the previous year's result is good and the current year's result is extremely good.

Exceptional items

You should always pay very close attention to expenditure or income labelled as exceptional. Look closely at the details given and ask yourself if it really was exceptional. Directors are sometimes criticised for being too ready to call bad news exceptional in order to flatter the underlying trend.

Rutland Robotics PLC had exceptional expenditure of £6,199,000 in 2001 and the use of the term appears to be absolutely correct. It was highly significant and without this expenditure the 2001 profit before tax would have been almost 50 per cent higher. You will notice that the explanation is given in note 2 and you will also notice that the directors' report says that the expenditure was necessary and successful. The improvement to the figures in 2002 seems to support this, athough one cannot always be certain about cause and effect.

The profit and loss account

Much ratio analysis entirely within the profit and loss account is both easy and useful. The following results for Rutland Robotics PLC can be readily obtained:

	Current year	Previous year
Profit before exceptional item to turnover	–	11.7%
Operating profit to turnover	17.6%	8.5%
Profit on ordinary activities before taxation to turnover	16.2%	6.7%
Profit on ordinary activities after taxation to turnover	12.0%	5.1%
Cost of sales to turnover	58.1%	63.2%
Gross profit to turnover	41.9%	36.8%
Net operating expenses to turnover	24.2%	25.1%
Interest payable to turnover	1.4%	1.8%
Interest payable to operating profit	8.2%	20.8%

All of this was explained on Monday and you should not find the calculations difficult. The next stage is more creative and perhaps not so simple. We shall now draw conclusions from the figures and frame questions that need answering.

Turnover analysis

This might be studied with the profit and loss account, but because separate information is given in the notes we will consider it separately. At first sight there is not much to say – just that turnover fell 2.2 per cent between the two years. However, a look at note 1 reveals a mine of information:

- Consultancy services contributed £12,187,000 (6.3 per cent) of the 2001 turnover. If this is stripped out, there is an increase of £6,897,000 (3.8 per cent) between the 2 years.
- There was a very significant increase in the share of turnover taken by the home market. The figures are:

	2002	**2001**
United Kingdom	79.2%	50.3%
Rest of the world	20.8%	49.7%

Unfortunately a separate geographical split is not given for the consultancy services division. This would have enabled us to see the exact split in 2001 for the continuing industrial machinery business. Despite this lack of information, the switch from exports to the home market is clearly very important. It may be a factor in the improvement to the gross profit margin. It is certainly worth looking at the directors' report to see if there is any explanation or comment on the subject.

Interest cover

This is an important and much studied ratio, especially when borrowing is high relative to shareholders' funds – a situation known as being highly geared. It is also particularly significant when the interest charge is high relative to profits.

Obviously a company that cannot pay its interest charge has severe problems and may not be able to carry on, at least not without a fresh injection of funds. The greater the interest cover, the greater the degree of safety.

Interest cover is profit before interest and tax, divided by the interest charge. It is important because interest must be paid if it is being incurred. The higher the number the more easily the company is managing to pay the interest charge. The figures for Rutland Robotics PLC are as follows:

	2002 £000s	2001 £000s
Profit before interest and tax	33,234	16,378
Interest charge	2,716	3,406
Interest cover	12.2	4.8

Taxation

Some analysts do not pay much attention to taxation. They take the view that taxes are more or less inevitable and take a more or less predictable share of pre-tax profits. This is an understandable viewpoint and the taxation of many companies does follow this pattern. However, it does not apply in all cases.

There may be some scope for the directors to limit the tax charge by skilful tax planning, although it is usually a mistake to do this at the expense of pre-tax profits. Company circumstances can make a difference, as can foreign taxes if they are applicable. Deferred tax and the timing of tax payments can be important. This may, for example, benefit companies with a large capital expenditure programme.

It can therefore be a mistake to ignore taxation. A key objective of most companies is to maximise after-tax profits. A £50,000 reduction in the tax charge contributes just as much to this end as a £50,000 reduction in the overheads.

The taxation charge of Rutland Robotics PLC is explained in note 4 and appears unexceptional. It is 25.9 per cent of the profit before tax in the current year and 24.0 per cent in the previous year. Note 4 shows an £88,000 tax charge relating to prior years. This should not be seen as unusual or alarming. It frequently takes several years to reach final agreement with the tax authorities.

The tax on profits should not be confused with VAT or other taxes. Amounts owing for these are shown in the creditors section of the balance sheet. Corporation tax charged against profits, but not yet paid over, is also shown here and details are given in note 9.

Dividend cover

What is dividend cover? As the catchphrase says – the answer is in the question. It is the number of times that the dividend is covered by the profit after tax. The calculations are:

Current year $\dfrac{22,605}{8,913} = 2.5$ to 1

Previous year $\dfrac{9,855}{8,913} = 1.1$ to 1

The greater the cover, the greater the margin of safety. Rutland Robotics PLC is paying relatively high dividends and, at first sight, the previous year dividend cover of 1.1 to 1 looks a little alarming. However, the company was well-financed and liquid, and the profit and loss account included an exceptional and non-recurring charge of £6,199,000. Presumably the directors looked forward to 2002 with confidence and, indeed, the results for 2002 show that this was not misplaced. For these reasons there is no cause for alarm and certainly no cause for concern about the 2002 dividend.

Summary

Today we have worked on the analysis of the published accounts of companies, concentrating mainly on the profit and loss account. We have:

- Discovered what to look for in the auditor's report
- Studied return on capital employed, which is possibly the most important ratio of all
- Looked at exceptional items, which can be very important
- Calculated the main profit and loss account ratios for Rutland Robotics PLC
- Looked at what information can be obtained about turnover
- Studied the important ratio of interest cover
- Considered the significance of taxation
- Examined dividend cover

Tomorrow we shall examine further the subject of the published accounts of companies, concentrating mainly on the balance sheet and the notes.

In-depth work with published accounts

Today we continue to analyse published accounts and once again we frequently refer to the accounts of Rutland Robotics PLC that were included in Wednesday's chapter. We concentrate mainly on the balance sheet and the notes and the programme is:

- Gearing
- Liquidity
- Stock and stock turn
- Fixed assets, depreciation and capital expenditure
- The notes to the accounts
- The directors' report

Gearing

This is the comparison between long-term lending by banks and others with the total shareholders' funds belonging to the owners of the company. It was explained on Tuesday and you will already be familiar with the principle.

Details of long-term borrowing can be found in note 10 and the amounts owing under hire purchase contracts will be omitted in these calculations, although you may decide to include them. Gearing in the current year is:

$$\frac{4,722}{51,976} = 9\% \text{ or } 0.9 \text{ to } 1$$

In the previous year it is:

$$\frac{7,282}{38,284} = 19\% \text{ or } 0.19 \text{ to } 1$$

The ratios in both years would normally be considered to be safe, conservative and unalarming, with a noticeable reduction between the two years. The main reason for this drop in the gearing ratio is the funds retained from a very profitable year.

Liquidity

This too should present no difficulties, because it was explained at length on Tuesday. A quick glance will show that there are no problems at all. Working capital at 31 December 2001 was an adequate £16,934,000 and at 31 December 2002 it was possibly more than adequate at £28,005,000.

This last point is a serious one. It is possible to have wastefully large working capital, although this is a problem that numerous companies would like to have. However, as there is still bank borrowing it would probably be a mistake to draw this conclusion. Moreover, the dramatic expansion plans outlined in the directors' report almost certainly indicate a call on working capital in the coming year. Even profitable large-scale expansion soaks up cash before the profits flow and the wait for customers to pay for the profitable invoicing is even longer. This is why rapidly expanding (but profitable) companies can be forced out of business.

The ratio calculations for Rutland Robotics PLC are as follows:

	Current year £000s	Previous year £000s
Current assets	53,722	47,932
Quick test assets	37,404	33,763
Current liabilities	25,717	30,998
Liquidity ratio	209%	155%
Quick ratio (acid test)	145%	109%

Stock and stock turn

Note 7 breaks down the total stock figures into the three categories most often used to show how stock is made up. It is noticeable that total stock increased by £2,149,000 or 15.2 per cent during the year. A more detailed look at the note shows that this was entirely caused by an increase in finished goods. These went up by £3,493,000 or 58.1 per cent. Raw materials were almost constant and work in progress reduced by £1,283,000 or 21.0 per cent.

This analysis does raise some very interesting questions – to which, of course, some very good answers may well be available. Questions include:

- Does the build up of finished goods indicate a problem in selling them?
- What proportion of the finished goods is covered by customers' orders?
- Why has work in progress fallen? Is it due to cutbacks implemented because of the increase in finished stock?

- Are we sure that all the stock is properly valued and that adequate stock reserves are in place?
- What has happened since the year end and are later figures available?

In view of the clear success of the company it is likely that convincing answers are available, but they are all legitimate questions. A full reading of the accounts package, especially the directors' report, may provide further information. As in so many cases, an insider is in a favourable position and will have more and better information.

Stock turn is the number of times that stock is used (turned over) in the course of a year. This was explained on Tuesday and, subject to some qualifications, a high figure indicates efficient operation. You should be aware that the result will be distorted if the stock figure in the balance sheet is not typical of the year as a whole. You should also be aware that the definition of cost of sales in the profit and loss account may not exactly conform with the way that finished stock is valued. Subject to this the stock turn figures are as follows:

	Current year £000s	Previous year £000s
Cost of sales	109,481	122,379
Stock	16,318	14,169
Stock turn	6.7	8.6

Fixed assets, depreciation and capital expenditure

The importance of these figures varies from company to company, but you will quickly realise from the size of the numbers that they are important to Rutland Robotics PLC. They can be an important factor in the cash statement, which will be explained tomorrow. Capital expenditure consumes cash but is not immediately reflected in the profit and loss account. On the other hand, depreciation is a non-cash charge to the profit and loss account.

Space does not allow for their inclusion here, but full details of the depreciation policies will be given in the accounts. They give the annual write-off rates for each class of asset and will be part of an overall statement about accounting policies. Depreciation policies do matter and you will readily appreciate that if different write-off rates are used, the result is a different declared profit. It has not happened in this case, but look for any change in depreciation policies. Any such changes must be disclosed, with the consequences for the declared profit.

Note 6 gives information about the fixed assets. You will see that £3,043,000 has been spent on fixed assets during the year and that fixed assets originally costing £1,079,000 were disposed of during the year. This figure of £1,079,000 is not the sale proceeds and a different amount will have been received. The difference between the amount received and the written down value will have been debited or credited to the profit or loss account, according to whether a surplus or deficit resulted.

The directors are required to disclose if, in their opinion, the real value of the fixed assets is materially different from the written down value in the accounts. They are also required to disclose details of any revaluations made during the year. Neither of these are applicable in this case.

You may or may not think it necessary to compare fixed assets with other figures in the balance sheet. If so, you can choose ratios that you think are helpful in the particular circumstances. Two possibilities (at 31 December 2002) are:

Fixed assets to total assets $\frac{29,062}{82,784} = 35\%$

Fixed assets to total net assets $\frac{29,062}{51,976} = 56\%$

You must use your judgement about whether this is good or bad. It depends on the company, the industry and the circumstances. The fact that Rutland Robotics PLC shows such a large figure for freehold land and buildings makes a big difference. Very different ratios would have been obtained if the premises had been rented.

The notes to the accounts

As stated earlier in this book, the notes to the accounts are usually very important and should not be neglected. Good analysts rarely make this mistake.

The number and complexity of the notes vary from company to company. Their purpose is to illuminate the figures in the accounts and give supporting details. You will probably find more notes than the ones given for Wednesday's example company. The following explains the notes from Wednesday that have not already been dealt with.

Dividends (note 5)

Details will be given of any interim dividends already paid and any final dividends proposed. Dividends on any preference shares are a fixed amount and must be paid, provided that the company has the money to do so. In this respect dividends are like interest. Interim dividends on ordinary shares are decided and paid by the directors.

Final dividends on ordinary shares are proposed by the directors and approved by the shareholders at the forthcoming general meeting. Not surprisingly, the shareholders usually do approve the proposed dividends.

A person analysing the accounts will want to be sure that the dividends can safely be afforded and that the company is not paying excessive amounts. If it is, preference dividends may be more of a problem because they probably cannot be stopped or suspended. Liquidity is very relevant and so is

dividend cover which was considered yesterday. You may well think that, if they can be afforded, high dividends are a good thing. They probably are, but you should consider whether or not the company is retaining enough funds to finance necessary and profitable investment.

Stocks (note 7)
This was considered earlier but it should be emphasised that it is helpful to look at the break-down as well as at the overall total. The basis of valuation should be stated in the accounts package and any change in the basis should be stated. This (if found) can be extremely important. As with depreciation, a change in accounting policy will produce a different profit.

Debtors and creditors (notes 8, 9 and 10)
We have looked at these but further reading will show that a number of different categories are given. It is not just trade debtors (customers) and trade creditors (suppliers). You will see that among others, bank overdraft, proposed dividend and corporation tax are listed. A bank overdraft is a creditor owing to the bank and it should not be forgotten that most bank overdrafts are repayable on demand.

The split of creditors into amounts owing within a year and after a year is required and it is an important distinction. Some creditors may be payable at a date that, although within a year, is some way in the future. Corporation tax is a possible example.

Directors (note 11)
Directors' remuneration gets much public attention, especially in relation to listed public companies. More information must be provided (in the notes and elsewhere) than is given for Rutland Robotics PLC. This includes the

names of all directors who held office during the year and, if they did not hold office for the whole year, the date of appointment and/or removal.

A listed public company will give details of the remuneration of each director and matters such as share options, bonuses and company-paid pension contributions. Information about any remuneration committee of the directors will be given.

You will probably want to keep an eye on directors' remuneration and form an opinion as to whether or not the amount is justified. Note 11 does show a very big increase and this may prompt some questions.

Staff numbers and costs (note 12)
A note will show the average number of employees in the year and it may break this down into different categories of staff. It will also show the total payroll cost during the year, with separate social security costs. It is a simple job to divide the number of people into the total cost to get an average cost per employee.

Note 12 is very interesting. The average number of employees fell by 305 (23 per cent), but 68 of these were as a result of the discontinued consultancy services division. The total payroll cost fell by £2,814,000 which is only 8 per cent. Directors pay is included in these figures and its increase will be one of the reasons that the fall is less than pro-rata. The information does suggest several questions that you may want to ask.

Contingent liability (note 13)

A contingent liability is one where the directors are aware that there is a possibility of a charge against the company but have decided to make no provision (or only a part-provision) in the accounts. They have not provided more because they do not believe that it is necessary to do so. Details are required to be given so that readers can ask questions and form their own conclusions.

The range of possibilities is huge. Contingent liabilities are frequently of minor significance but, as with note 13, they can relate to big amounts. In this case you should certainly take note of what is said and perhaps ask questions. The directors firmly use the phrase *'believe that the claim has no validity whatsoever'* and this is very reassuring, but what if they are wrong? The amount in question is big enough to hurt.

Capital commitments (note 14)

These are binding contractual commitments for future capital expenditure. They are not shown in the accounts and the amounts involved may be trivial or significant. The total amount committed must be stated and it may be important, not least because of the implication for future depreciation and future cash resources. The amounts disclosed in note 14 are indeed worth noting.

The directors' report

Certain information must be given in the directors' report if it is applicable to the company. It is a long list that includes:

- A fair review of the development of the business of the company and its subsidiaries during the period, and the position at the end of the period.
- With minor exceptions, details of expenditure for political or charitable purposes.
- Details of any important events since the year end, an indication of likely future developments of the business, and an indication of the activities in research and development.
- Any difference in the market value of interests in land or buildings over book value at the balance sheet date, if directors consider that members' attention should be drawn to it. In practice, this is usually only done if the difference is material.
- Details of each director's interest in shares or debentures at the beginning and end of the year. Interest in the shares or debentures of any other group company must also be stated, as must the interest of any immediate family member and any options or rights to subscribe for shares or debentures.
- Details of the principal activities and any changes in these during the year.

It will be seen that the extract from the directors' report of Rutland Robotics PLC is only a small part of the complete document. However, it is a bombshell, and you should give it a great deal of attention. The report baldly states an intention to double both profits and turnover within 2 years. This sounds splendid and will be if achieved, but it should provoke many questions incorporating phrases like, How? Where? When? Can we really? Are you sure? What if? Some of these questions may be answered elsewhere in the report. Remember that accounts are backward-looking documents that tell you what has happened. This is very important, but it is also necessary to look to the future.

Summary

Today we have continued our work on the analysis of the published accounts of companies. We have concentrated on the balance sheet, notes to the accounts and the directors' report. We have:

- Renewed our acquaintance with the vital ratios for gearing, liquidity and stock turn
- Looked closely at the linked subjects of fixed assets, depreciation and capital expenditure
- Considered the function of notes to the accounts and looked at several key examples
- Had a first proper look at the directors' report, seen some of the subjects that are included in it and highlighted the importance of looking forwards as well as backwards

Tomorrow we will look at analysis and ratios that are particularly relevant for investment decisions, and we shall examine cash statements and associated matters. We will then round off the whole week with some questions that cover the topics that we have studied during the last seven days.

Cash and investment ratios

Our work finishes with two separate subjects. First of all we look at analysis involving the cash flow statement and we then move on to work with investment ratios. We conclude with some questions for you to test your understanding of all that you have done during the week. Today we shall look at:

- Cash flow statement
- Introduction to investment ratios
- Dividend per share
- Dividend yield
- Earnings per share
- Price earnings ratio
- A test for the week

Cash flow statement

An example of a cash flow statement appears below. This statement is compulsory for companies of a certain size and the content and layout must conform with recognised accounting principles. At first sight it can appear confusing, and you may find it the most difficult to understand of all the financial statements. Space does not permit inclusion here, but usually nearly all the figures will be explained by supporting notes.

Cash and profit are two separate things. It is quite possible, and indeed common, for a company to declare an accounting profit but to suffer a net cash outflow over the period. The reverse is also both possible and common. The reasons for this include:

- Non-cash items in the profit and loss account such as depreciation and bad debt reserves
- Customers paying more slowly or more quickly
- Suppliers being paid more slowly or more quickly
- Taxation
- Payment of dividends
- Capital expenditure

A cash flow statement identifies the net increase or net decrease in cash during the period, and it identifies the factors that contribute to this figure. In the following example there has been a net increase of £56,500 during the current year. It is notable that this is more than accounted for by the income from acquisitions and disposals. The section at the bottom reconciles the statement to the net debt at the balance sheet date, and the net debt figure is taken from figures in the balance sheet.

Deftrab Ltd
Cash Flow Statement for the Year
to 31 December 2002

	2002 £000	2001 £000
Operating activities		
Received from customers	824.1	796.5
Payments to suppliers	(506.8)	(531.2)
Payments to and on behalf of employees	(111.7)	(123.7)
Other payments	(61.4)	(72.6)
Cash inflow from operating activities	144.2	69.0
Taxation	(31.6)	(19.9)
Capital expenditure	(22.7)	(26.8)
Acquisitions and disposals	61.6	(13.3)
Equity dividends paid	(42.7)	(22.9)
Cash inflow/(outflow) before financing	108.8	(13.9)
Financing	(52.3)	(58.4)
Increase/(decrease) in cash	56.5	(72.3)

Reconciliation of net cash flow to movement in debt

	2002 £000	2001 £000
Increase/(decrease) in cash	56.5	(72.3)
Cash (inflow)/outflow from (decrease)/ increase in liquid resources	(79.2)	100.0
Cash outflow/(inflow) from decrease/ (increase) in debt financing	91.4	(39.8)
Movement in net debt	68.7	(12.1)
Net debt at 1 January	(638.0)	(625.9)
Net debt at 31 December	(569.3)	(638.0)

The cash flow statement is important and professional analysts always give it a great deal of attention. It is extremely difficult (or perhaps impossible) to manipulate and it delivers a hard uncompromising message. Cash is either present or it is absent. There may be much more scope for 'massaging' (possibly with good intentions) the profit and loss account. Cash is fact, whereas profit may be a matter of opinion. It is interesting to look back over the published accounts of some well-known company failures. The cash flow statements almost always indicated the deteriorating position although, in some cases, the profit and loss accounts showed a more cheerful situation.

When analysing a cash flow statement, it is a good idea to look first at the overall increase or decrease in cash. If there is an increase, you should note the reasons. If there is a decrease you should know why and form an opinion about whether the reason is a good one or a bad one. There may of course be an excellent reason, such as planned and profitable capital investment.

You will be interested to see precisely how the company is financed and this information should be available in the reconciliation section at the bottom. Bank borrowing is a constituent part of 'debt financing'.

The analysis and questions to ask will depend on the headings used and on the figures. You should look at the headings that are outside the scope of operating activities. Are any of them particularly significant in relation to the totals? Capital expenditure and also acquisitions and disposals may be extremely important.

Introduction to investment ratios

One of the most common reasons for analysing accounts is to help make investment decisions. It is therefore fitting that investment ratios should be the final subject examined this week. Everything that you have studied so far is relevant to investment decisions, but please take a few minutes to look at the following four frequently used investment ratios. Examples draw on the accounts of Rutland Robotics PLC which were included in Wednesday's chapter.

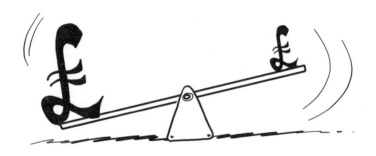

Dividend per share

Dividend per share is the total dividend divided by the number of issued shares. Care should be taken to see that the number of shares is the number of equity shares. Preference shares are normally excluded from the calculation. A note to the accounts will give the number of shares in issue. Take care to use the number of issued shares rather than the number of authorised shares, which will also be given. The nominal value of the shares is irrelevant.

Note 5 to the accounts of Rutland Robotics PLC gives the dividend per share. As the dividend is £8,913,000 and as the dividend per share is 43.2p, it follows that the shares in issue must be 20,630,000 (number rounded).

There is no point in comparing dividend per share between different companies. It may, however, be useful to plot dividend per share in the same company over a period.

Dividend yield

Dividend yield, unlike dividend per share, can usefully be compared between companies. It is the dividend expressed as a percentage of the current share price. Put another way it is:

$$\frac{\text{Dividend yield} \times 100}{\text{Quoted price per share}}$$

If the current quoted price per share of Rutland Robotics PLC is £10, the dividend yield will be:

$$\frac{43.2 \times 100}{1000} = 4.3\%$$

Earnings per share

This is net profit after tax divided by the number of issued shares. Once again there is no point in comparing this between different companies, but it is extremely useful to plot the trend over a period within a single company.

The current year calculation for Rutland Robotics PLC is:

$$\frac{£22,605,000}{20,630,000} = £1.10$$

and for the previous year it is:

$$\frac{£9,855,000}{20,630,000} = 48p$$

This takes no account of the exceptional item and you might want to add this back. If so, the prior year calculation is:

$$\frac{£16,054,000}{20,630,000} = 78p$$

Price earnings ratio

This is one of the most helpful of the investment ratios and it can be used to compare different companies. It is often utilised to make a judgement about whether a particular company's shares are relatively cheap or relatively expensive. The higher the number, the more expensive the shares. It is often useful to do the calculation based on anticipated future earnings rather than declared historic earnings. Of course you cannot always, or indeed ever, be certain what future earnings will be.

The calculation is quoted price per share divided by earnings per share. In the case of Rutland Robotics PLC this is:

$$\frac{£10.00}{£1.10} = 9.1$$

This seems a low number so perhaps the shares are worth buying, but on the other hand perhaps the market does not have faith in the company's expansion plans.

A test for the week

Our work is over and hopefully you are feeling confident. We will now put your knowledge to the test with some questions that cover all 7 days. The questions follow extracts from a set of accounts and can be answered by analysing them.

Information from the profit and loss account

Turnover	£100,000,000
Gross profit	£30,000,000
Profit on ordinary activities before taxation	£5,000,000
Profit on ordinary activities after taxation	£3,700,000

Information from the balance sheet

Current assets	£61,000,000
Total of debtors, investments, bank and cash	£47,000,000
Current liabilities	£52,000,000
Total long-term bank borrowing	£40,000,000
Shareholders' funds	£60,000,000

Other available information

Total trade debtors	£13,000,000
Number of shares issued	30,000,000
Current share price	£2.57

(The answers to this section are given at the end of the book.)

1 What is the cost of sales expressed as a percentage?
2 What is the net profit margin, using profit before tax?
3 What is the profit margin, using profit after tax?
4 What is the working capital?
5 What is the quick ratio (acid test)?
6 What is the average number of days credit taken by customers? Ignore a possible VAT complication.
7 What is the gearing ratio (using just long-term bank borrowing)?
8 What is the earnings per share?
9 What is the price earnings ratio?

Summary

Today we have studied the cash flow statement and also various investment ratios. They are not the easiest subjects but they are among the most valuable. We have:

- Seen the importance of a cash flow statement and how it may be used
- Examined the detailed layout of a cash flow statement
- Looked at four important and commonly used investment ratios
- Ended the week with some relevant questions. Hopefully they gave you little trouble and you enjoyed answering the

Answers to practical questions

Questions asked on Monday

1 0.2% $\left(\dfrac{14,149}{8,137,371}\right)$

2 20.0%. This is 44.3% $\left(\dfrac{2,762,303}{6,241.452}\right)$ less 22.3% $\left(\dfrac{1,814,086}{1,814,086}\right)$

3 2002 is 48.7% $\left(\dfrac{3,961,258}{8,137,371}\right)$

  2001 is 32.2% $\left(\dfrac{2,009,784}{6,241,452}\right)$

4 Overheads have increased by 1.5% in relation to sales.
  2002 is 19.3% $\left(\dfrac{1,573,436}{8,137,371}\right)$; 2001 is 17.8% $\left(\dfrac{1,111,126}{6,241,452}\right)$

5 More than one answer is possible but the following are suggested.

  - Cost of sales has increased from 55.7% to 77.7%

  - Overheads have increased from 17.8% of sales to 19.3% of sales with the increase in publicity being particularly noticeable

  - Interest has increased from 0.8% of sales to 2.7% of sales

6 There is not enough information to say, although it may be the case. The decline in profits may be unconnected or it may be part of a successful long-term plan.

Questions asked on Tuesday

1 £131,282

2 $\dfrac{2{,}453{,}345}{3{,}163{,}847} = 78\%$

3 $\dfrac{1{,}500{,}000}{5{,}523{,}515} = 27\%$

3 No

5 $\dfrac{7{,}621{,}389}{841{,}784} = 9.1$

6 $\dfrac{2{,}039{,}245}{12{,}199{,}318} \times 365 = 61$ days

7 $\dfrac{1{,}162{,}975}{8{,}318{,}199} \times 365 = 51$ days

Questions asked on Wednesday

Test your understanding
1 Directors' report
2 Profit and loss account
3 Balance sheet
4 Cash flow information
5 Notes to the accounts
6 Notes to the accounts
7 Directors' report

Do you remember Monday and Tuesday?

1   £16,934,000

2 $\dfrac{30,998}{33,763} = 0.92$ to 1

3 $\dfrac{12,972}{193,616} = 6.7\%$

4 $\dfrac{48,660}{193,616} = 25.1\%$

Questions asked on Saturday

1 $\dfrac{70,000,000}{100,000,000} = 70\%$

The cost of sales is £70,000,000 (The difference between the turnover of 100,000,000 and gross profit of £30,000,000).

2 $\dfrac{5,000,000}{100,000,000} = 5.0\%$

3 $\dfrac{3,700,000}{100,000,000} = 3.7\%$

4 £61,000,000 less £52,000,000 = £9,000,000

5 $\dfrac{47,000,000}{52,000,000} = 90\%$ or 0.9 to 1

6 $\dfrac{13,000,000}{100,000,000} \times 365 = 47$ days

7 $\dfrac{40,000,000}{60,000,000} = 66\%$ or 0.7 to 1

8 $\dfrac{3,700,000}{30,000,000} = 12.3\text{p}$

9 $\dfrac{\text{£}2.57}{12.3\text{p}} = 20.9$

For information

on other

IN A WEEK titles

go to

www.inaweek.co.uk